THIS JOURNAL BELONGS TO:

_____

Copyright © 2021 Kinvara Creative

All rights reserved.

To the incredible teachers who make a difference in the lives of so many: May the practice of cultivating gratitude bring you joy and peace.

Date: _____

One moment that brought me happiness today:
_____
_____
_____

One moment that I don't want to forget:
_____
_____
_____

> "BE GRATEFUL IN YOUR OWN HEARTS. THAT SUFFICES. THANKSGIVING HAS WINGS, AND FLIES TO ITS RIGHT DESTINATION." — VICTOR HUGO

Date: _____

One moment that gave me confidence today:
_____
_____
_____

One moment I am grateful for today:
_____
_____
_____

Date: _____

One moment that brought me peace today:
_____
_____
_____

One moment that I don't want to forget:
_____
_____
_____

> "THE DUTIES OF A TEACHER ARE NEITHER FEW NOR SMALL, BUT THEY ELEVATE THE MIND AND GIVE ENERGY TO THE CHARACTER" — DOROTHEA DIX

Date: _____

One moment that made me laugh:
_____
_____
_____

One moment I am grateful for today:
_____
_____
_____

Date: _____

One moment that brought me comfort today:
_____
_____
_____

One moment that I don't want to forget:
_____
_____
_____

"THE BEST TEACHERS ARE THOSE WHO SHOW YOU WHERE TO LOOK BUT DON'T TELL YOU WHAT TO SEE." — ALEXANDRA K. TRENFOR

Date: _____

One dream I have for my family is:
_____
_____
_____

One moment I am grateful for today:
_____
_____
_____

Date: _____

One moment that gave me hope today:
_____
_____
_____

One moment that I don't want to forget:
_____
_____
_____

> "ANYONE WHO DOES ANYTHING TO HELP A CHILD IN HIS LIFE IS A HERO." — FRED ROGERS

Date: _____

One moment that I am proud of:
_____
_____
_____

One moment I am grateful for today:
_____
_____
_____

Date: _____

One moment that gave me confidence today:
_____
_____
_____

One moment that I don't want to forget:
_____
_____
_____

> "GRATITUDE GOES BEYOND THE 'MINE' AND 'THINE' AND CLAIMS THE TRUTH THAT ALL OF LIFE IS A PURE GIFT." — HENRI NOUWEN

Date: _____

One moment that brought me peace today:
_____
_____
_____

One moment I am grateful for today:
_____
_____

Date: _____

One moment that made me smile:
_____
_____
_____

One moment that I don't want to forget:
_____
_____
_____

> "GRATITUDE IS A POWERFUL CATALYST FOR HAPPINESS. IT'S THE SPARK THAT LIGHTS A FIRE OF JOY IN YOUR SOUL." — AMY COLLETTE

Date: _____

One moment that brought me joy today:
_____
_____
_____

One moment I am grateful for today:
_____
_____
_____

Date: _____

One moment that made me laugh:
_____
_____
_____

One moment that I don't want to forget:
_____
_____
_____

"EDUCATION IS NOT THE FILLING OF A PAIL BUT THE LIGHTING OF A FIRE." — W.B. YEATS

Date: _____

One moment that brought me happiness today:
_____
_____
_____

One moment I am grateful for today:
_____
_____
_____

Date: _____

One moment that I am proud of:
_____
_____
_____

One moment that I don't want to forget:
_____
_____
_____

> "IT'S A FUNNY THING ABOUT LIFE, ONCE YOU BEGIN TO TAKE NOTE OF THE THINGS YOU ARE GRATEFUL FOR, YOU BEGIN TO LOSE SIGHT OF THE THINGS THAT YOU LACK." — GERMANY KENT

Date: _____

One moment that gave me hope today:
_____
_____
_____

One moment I am grateful for today:
_____
_____
_____

Date: _____

One dream I have for my family is:
_____
_____
_____

One moment that I don't want to forget:
_____
_____
_____

> "TEACHING KIDS TO COUNT IS FINE, BUT TEACHING THEM WHAT COUNTS IS BEST." — BOB TALBERT

Date: _____

One moment that made me smile:
_____
_____
_____

One moment I am grateful for today:
_____
_____
_____

Date: _____

One moment that brought me joy today:
_____
_____
_____

One moment that I don't want to forget:
_____
_____
_____

> "TELL ME AND I FORGET. TEACH ME AND I REMEMBER. INVOLVE ME AND I LEARN."
> — BENJAMIN FRANKLIN

Date: _____

One moment that brought me comfort today:
_____
_____
_____

One moment I am grateful for today:
_____
_____
_____

Date: _____

One moment that brought me happiness today:
_____
_____
_____

One moment that I don't want to forget:
_____
_____
_____

"ENJOY THE LITTLE THINGS, FOR ONE DAY YOU MAY LOOK BACK AND REALIZE THEY WERE THE BIG THINGS." — ROBERT BRAULT

Date: _____

One moment that gave me confidence today:
_____
_____
_____

One moment I am grateful for today:
_____
_____
_____

Date: _____

One moment that brought me peace today:
_____
_____
_____

One moment that I don't want to forget:
_____
_____
_____

> "WHEN WE FOCUS ON OUR GRATITUDE, THE TIDE OF DISAPPOINTMENT GOES OUT AND THE TIDE OF LOVE RUSHES IN." – KRISTIN ARMSTRONG

Date: _____

One moment that made me laugh:
_____
_____
_____

One moment I am grateful for today:
_____
_____
_____

Date: _____

One moment that brought me comfort today:
_____
_____
_____

One moment that I don't want to forget:
_____
_____
_____

"WEAR GRATITUDE LIKE A CLOAK, AND IT WILL FEED EVERY CORNER OF YOUR LIFE." – RUMI

Date: _____

One dream I have for my family is:
_____
_____
_____

One moment I am grateful for today:
_____
_____
_____

Date: _____

One moment that gave me hope today:
_____
_____
_____

One moment that I don't want to forget:
_____
_____
_____

> "GRATITUDE TURNS WHAT WE HAVE INTO ENOUGH, AND MORE. IT TURNS DENIAL INTO ACCEPTANCE, CHAOS INTO ORDER, CONFUSION INTO CLARITY...IT MAKES SENSE OF OUR PAST, BRINGS PEACE FOR TODAY, AND CREATES A VISION FOR TOMORROW." — MELODY BEATTIE

Date: _____

One moment that I am proud of:
_____
_____
_____

One moment I am grateful for today:
_____
_____
_____

Date: _____

One moment that gave me confidence today:
_____
_____
_____

One moment that I don't want to forget:
_____
_____
_____

"NINE-TENTHS OF EDUCATION IS ENCOURAGEMENT." — ANATOLE FRANCE

Date: _____

One moment that brought me peace today:
_____
_____
_____

One moment I am grateful for today:
_____
_____
_____

Date: _____

One moment that made me smile:
_____
_____
_____

One moment that I don't want to forget:
_____
_____
_____

> "TEACHERS HAVE THREE LOVES: LOVE OF LEARNING, LOVE OF LEARNERS, AND THE LOVE OF BRINGING THE FIRST TWO LOVES TOGETHER."
> — SCOTT HAYDEN

Date: _____

One moment that brought me joy today:
_____
_____
_____

One moment I am grateful for today:
_____
_____
_____

Date: _____

One moment that made me laugh:
_____
_____
_____

One moment that I don't want to forget:
_____
_____
_____

"EDUCATION IS OUR PASSPORT TO THE FUTURE, FOR TOMORROW BELONGS TO THE PEOPLE WHO PREPARE FOR IT TODAY." — MALCOLM X

Date: _____

One moment that brought me happiness today:
_____
_____
_____

One moment I am grateful for today:
_____
_____
_____

Date: _____

One moment that I am proud of:
_____
_____
_____

One moment that I don't want to forget:
_____
_____
_____

> "IF YOU FAIL TO CARRY AROUND WITH YOU
> A HEART OF GRATITUDE FOR THE LOVE YOU'VE
> BEEN SO FREELY GIVEN, IT IS EASY FOR YOU
> NOT TO LOVE OTHERS AS YOU SHOULD."
> — PAUL DAVID TRIPP

Date: _____

One moment that gave me hope today:
_____
_____
_____

One moment I am grateful for today:
_____
_____
_____

Date: _____

One dream I have for my family is:
_____
_____
_____

One moment that I don't want to forget:
_____
_____
_____

"THE ART OF TEACHING IS THE ART OF ASSISTING DISCOVERY." — MARK VAN DOREN

Date: _____

One moment that made me smile:
_____
_____
_____

One moment I am grateful for today:
_____
_____
_____

Date: _____

One moment that brought me joy today:
_____
_____
_____

One moment that I don't want to forget:
_____
_____
_____

"JOY IS THE SIMPLEST FORM OF GRATITUDE."
— KARL BARTH

Date: _____

One moment that brought me comfort today:
_____
_____
_____

One moment I am grateful for today:
_____
_____
_____

Date: _____

One moment that brought me happiness today:
_____
_____
_____

One moment that I don't want to forget:
_____
_____
_____

"TO TEACH IS TO LEARN TWICE OVER."
— JOSEPH JOUBERT

Date: _____

One moment that gave me confidence today:
_____
_____
_____

One moment I am grateful for today:
_____
_____
_____

Date: _____

One moment that brought me peace today:
_____
_____
_____

One moment that I don't want to forget:
_____
_____
_____

> "A TEACHER AFFECTS ETERNITY; HE CAN NEVER TELL WHERE HIS INFLUENCE STOPS." — HENRY B. ADAMS

Date: _____

One moment that made me laugh:
_____
_____
_____

One moment I am grateful for today:
_____
_____
_____

Date: _____

One moment that brought me comfort today:
_____
_____
_____

One moment that I don't want to forget:
_____
_____
_____

> "I THINK GRATITUDE IS A BIG THING. IT PUTS YOU IN A PLACE WHERE YOU'RE HUMBLE." — ANDRA DAY

Date: _____

One dream I have for my family is:
_____
_____
_____

One moment I am grateful for today:
_____
_____

Date: _____

One moment that gave me hope today:
_____
_____
_____

One moment that I don't want to forget:
_____
_____
_____

> "APPRECIATION IS A WONDERFUL THING. IT MAKES WHAT IS EXCELLENT IN OTHERS BELONG TO US AS WELL." — VOLTAIRE

Date: _____

One moment that I am proud of:
_____
_____
_____

One moment I am grateful for today:
_____
_____
_____

Date: _____

One moment that gave me confidence today:
_____
_____
_____

One moment that I don't want to forget:
_____
_____
_____

> "THEY MAY FORGET WHAT YOU SAID BUT THEY WILL NOT FORGET HOW YOU MADE THEM FEEL."
> — CARL BUECHNER

Date: _____

One moment that brought me peace today:
_____
_____
_____

One moment I am grateful for today:
_____
_____

Date: _____

One moment that made me smile:
_____
_____
_____

One moment that I don't want to forget:
_____
_____
_____

> "ALL STUDENTS CAN LEARN AND SUCCEED, BUT NOT IN THE SAME WAY AND NOT IN THE SAME DAY." — WILLIAM G. SPADY

Date: _____

One moment that brought me joy today:
_____
_____
_____

One moment I am grateful for today:
_____
_____
_____

Date: _____

One moment that made me laugh:
_____
_____
_____

One moment that I don't want to forget:
_____
_____
_____

"'ENOUGH' IS A FEAST." — BUDDHIST PROVERB

Date: _____

One moment that brought me happiness today:
_____
_____
_____

One moment I am grateful for today:
_____
_____
_____

Date: _____

One moment that I am proud of:
_____
_____
_____

One moment that I don't want to forget:
_____
_____
_____

> "LET US BE GRATEFUL TO THE PEOPLE WHO MAKE US HAPPY; THEY ARE THE CHARMING GARDENERS WHO MAKE OUR SOULS BLOSSOM."
> — MARCEL PROUST

Date: _____

One moment that gave me hope today:
_____
_____
_____

One moment I am grateful for today:
_____
_____
_____

Date: _____

One dream I have for my family is:
_____
_____
_____

One moment that I don't want to forget:
_____
_____
_____

> "I LIKE A TEACHER WHO GIVES YOU SOMETHING TO TAKE HOME TO THINK ABOUT BESIDES HOMEWORK"
> — LILY TOMLIN

Date: _____

One moment that made me smile:
_____
_____
_____

One moment I am grateful for today:
_____
_____

Date: _____

One moment that brought me joy today:
_____
_____
_____

One moment that I don't want to forget:
_____
_____
_____

> "CULTIVATE THE HABIT OF BEING GRATEFUL FOR EVERY GOOD THING THAT COMES TO YOU, AND TO GIVE THANKS CONTINUOUSLY. YOU SHOULD INCLUDE ALL THINGS IN YOUR GRATITUDE."
> – RALPH WALDO EMERSON

Date: _____

One moment that brought me comfort today:
_____
_____
_____

One moment I am grateful for today:
_____
_____
_____

Date: _____

One moment that brought me happiness today:
_____
_____
_____

One moment that I don't want to forget:
_____
_____
_____

"GRATITUDE IS NOT ONLY THE GREATEST OF VIRTUES, BUT THE PARENT OF ALL OTHERS."
— MARCUS TULLIUS CICERO

Date: _____

One moment that gave me confidence today:
_____
_____
_____

One moment I am grateful for today:
_____
_____
_____

Date: _____

One moment that brought me peace today:
_____
_____
_____

One moment that I don't want to forget:
_____
_____
_____

> "WE MUST FIND TIME TO STOP AND THANK THE PEOPLE WHO MAKE A DIFFERENCE IN OUR LIVES."
> — JOHN F. KENNEDY

Date: _____

One moment that made me laugh:
_____
_____
_____

One moment I am grateful for today:
_____
_____
_____

Date: _____

One moment that brought me comfort today:
_____
_____
_____

One moment that I don't want to forget:
_____
_____
_____

> "TECHNOLOGY IS JUST A TOOL. IN TERMS OF GETTING THE KIDS TO WORK TOGETHER AND MOTIVATING THEM, THE TEACHER IS THE MOST IMPORTANT." — BILL GATES

Date: _____

One dream I have for my family is:
_____
_____
_____

One moment I am grateful for today:
_____
_____
_____

Date: _____

One moment that gave me hope today:
_____
_____
_____

One moment that I don't want to forget:
_____
_____
_____

> "THE HEART THAT GIVES THANKS IS A HAPPY ONE, FOR WE CANNOT FEEL THANKFUL AND UNHAPPY AT THE SAME TIME." — DOUGLAS WOOD

Date: _____

One moment that I am proud of:
_____
_____
_____

One moment I am grateful for today:
_____
_____
_____

Date: _____

One moment that gave me confidence today:
_____
_____
_____

One moment that I don't want to forget:
_____
_____
_____

"ALWAYS HAVE AN ATTITUDE OF GRATITUDE."
— STERLING K. BROWN

Date: _____

One moment that brought me peace today:
_____
_____
_____

One moment I am grateful for today:
_____
_____
_____

Date: _____

One moment that made me smile:
_____
_____
_____

One moment that I don't want to forget:
_____
_____
_____

"IT'S THE TEACHER THAT MAKES THE DIFFERENCE, NOT THE CLASSROOM." — MICHAEL MORPURGO

Date: _____

One moment that brought me joy today:
_____
_____
_____

One moment I am grateful for today:
_____
_____
_____

Date: _____

One moment that made me laugh:
_____
_____
_____

One moment that I don't want to forget:
_____
_____
_____

"GOOD TEACHING IS ONE-FOURTH PREPARATION AND THREE-FOURTHS THEATRE." — GAIL GOLDWIN

Date: _____

One moment that brought me happiness today:
_____
_____
_____

One moment I am grateful for today:
_____
_____
_____

Date: _____

One moment that I am proud of:
_____
_____
_____

One moment that I don't want to forget:
_____
_____
_____

> "I AM HAPPY BECAUSE I'M GRATEFUL. I CHOOSE TO BE GRATEFUL. THAT GRATITUDE ALLOWS ME TO BE HAPPY." — WILL ARNETT

Date: _____

One moment that gave me hope today:
_____
_____
_____

One moment I am grateful for today:
_____
_____
_____

Date: _____

One dream I have for my family is:
_____
_____
_____

One moment that I don't want to forget:
_____
_____
_____

"EVERYONE WHO REMEMBERS HIS OWN EDUCATION REMEMBERS TEACHERS, NOT METHODS AND TECHNIQUES. THE TEACHER IS THE HEART OF THE EDUCATIONAL SYSTEM." — SIDNEY HOOK

Date: _____

One moment that made me smile:
_____
_____
_____

One moment I am grateful for today:
_____
_____
_____

Date: _____

One moment that brought me joy today:
_____
_____
_____

One moment that I don't want to forget:
_____
_____
_____

> "THE TASK OF THE MODERN EDUCATOR IS NOT TO CUT DOWN JUNGLES, BUT TO IRRIGATE DESERTS."
> — C.S. LEWIS

Date: _____

One moment that brought me comfort today:
_____
_____
_____

One moment I am grateful for today:
_____
_____
_____

Date: _____

One moment that brought me happiness today:
_____
_____
_____

One moment that I don't want to forget:
_____
_____
_____

"I TOUCH THE FUTURE. I TEACH."
— CHRISTA MCAULIFFE

Date: _____

One moment that gave me confidence today:
_____
_____
_____

One moment I am grateful for today:
_____
_____
_____

Date: _____

One moment that brought me peace today:
_____
_____
_____

One moment that I don't want to forget:
_____
_____
_____

"NO DUTY IS MORE URGENT THAN GIVING THANKS." — JAMES ALLEN

Date: _____

One moment that made me laugh:
_____
_____
_____

One moment I am grateful for today:
_____
_____
_____

Date: _____

One moment that brought me comfort today:
_____
_____
_____

One moment that I don't want to forget:
_____
_____
_____

"I AM A TEACHER BORN AND BRED, AND I BELIEVE IN THE ADVOCACY OF TEACHERS. IT'S A CALLING. WE WANT OUR STUDENTS TO FEEL IMPASSIONED AND EMPOWERED." — ERIN GRUWELL

Date: _____

One dream I have for my family is:
_____
_____
_____

One moment I am grateful for today:
_____
_____
_____

Date: _____

One moment that gave me hope today:
_____
_____
_____

One moment that I don't want to forget:
_____
_____
_____

> "IF YOU HAVE TO PUT SOMEONE ON A PEDESTAL, PUT TEACHERS. THEY ARE SOCIETY'S HEROES."
> — GUY KAWASAKI

Date: _____

One moment that I am proud of:
_____
_____
_____

One moment I am grateful for today:
_____
_____
_____

Date: _____

One moment that gave me confidence today:
_____
_____
_____

One moment that I don't want to forget:
_____
_____
_____

"GRATITUDE IS THE ABILITY TO EXPERIENCE LIFE AS A GIFT. IT LIBERATES US FROM THE PRISON OF SELF-PREOCCUPATION." — JOHN ORTBERG

Date: _____

One moment that brought me peace today:
_____
_____
_____

One moment I am grateful for today:
_____
_____
_____

Date: _____

One moment that made me smile:
_____
_____
_____

One moment that I don't want to forget:
_____
_____
_____

> "AS WE EXPRESS OUR GRATITUDE, WE MUST NEVER FORGET THAT THE HIGHEST APPRECIATION IS NOT TO UTTER WORDS, BUT TO LIVE BY THEM."
> — JOHN F. KENNEDY

Date: _____

One moment that brought me joy today:
_____
_____
_____

One moment I am grateful for today:
_____
_____
_____

Date: _____

One moment that made me laugh:
_____
_____
_____

One moment that I don't want to forget:
_____
_____
_____

> "TO THIS END, THE GREATEST ASSET OF A SCHOOL IS THE PERSONALITY OF THE TEACHER."
> — JOHN STRACHAN

Date: _____

One moment that brought me happiness today:
_____
_____
_____

One moment I am grateful for today:
_____
_____
_____

Date: _____

One moment that I am proud of:
_____
_____
_____

One moment that I don't want to forget:
_____
_____
_____

> "THE WHOLE PURPOSE OF EDUCATION IS TO TURN MIRRORS INTO WINDOWS." — SYDNEY J. HARRIS

Date: _____

One moment that gave me hope today:
_____
_____
_____

One moment I am grateful for today:
_____
_____
_____

Date: _____

One dream I have for my family is:
_____
_____
_____

One moment that I don't want to forget:
_____
_____
_____

> "THE UNTHANKFUL HEART DISCOVERS NO MERCIES; BUT THE THANKFUL HEART WILL FIND, IN EVERY HOUR, SOME HEAVENLY BLESSINGS."
> — HENRY WARD BEECHER

Date: _____

One moment that made me smile:
_____
_____
_____

One moment I am grateful for today:
_____
_____
_____

Date: _____

One moment that brought me joy today:
_____
_____
_____

One moment that I don't want to forget:
_____
_____
_____

> "WHEN IT COMES TO LIFE, THE CRITICAL THING IS WHETHER YOU TAKE THINGS FOR GRANTED OR TAKE THEM WITH GRATITUDE." — G.K. CHESTERON

Date: _____

One moment that brought me comfort today:
_____
_____
_____

One moment I am grateful for today:
_____
_____
_____

Date: _____

One moment that brought me happiness today:
_____
_____
_____

One moment that I don't want to forget:
_____
_____
_____

"GRATITUDE AND ATTITUDE ARE NOT CHALLENGES; THEY ARE CHOICES." — ROBERT BRAATHE

Date: _____

One moment that gave me confidence today:
_____
_____
_____

One moment I am grateful for today:
_____
_____
_____

Date: _____

One moment that brought me peace today:
_____
_____
_____

One moment that I don't want to forget:
_____
_____
_____

> "WHAT SCULPTURE IS TO A BLOCK OF MARBLE, EDUCATION IS TO A HUMAN SOUL."
> — JOSEPH ADDISON

Date: _____

One moment that made me laugh:
_____
_____
_____

One moment I am grateful for today:
_____
_____
_____

Date: _____

One moment that brought me comfort today:
_____
_____
_____

One moment that I don't want to forget:
_____
_____
_____

> "WE CAN ONLY BE SAID TO BE ALIVE IN THOSE MOMENTS WHEN OUR HEARTS ARE CONSCIOUS OF OUR TREASURES." — THORNTON WILDER

Date: _____

One dream I have for my family is:
_____
_____
_____

One moment I am grateful for today:
_____
_____
_____

Date: _____

One moment that gave me hope today:
_____
_____
_____

One moment that I don't want to forget:
_____
_____
_____

"EDUCATION BREEDS CONFIDENCE. CONFIDENCE BREEDS HOPE. HOPE BREEDS PEACE." — CONFUCIUS

Date: _____

One moment that I am proud of:
_____
_____
_____

One moment I am grateful for today:
_____
_____
_____

Date: _____

One moment that gave me confidence today:
_____
_____
_____

One moment that I don't want to forget:
_____
_____
_____

"WHEN YOU ARISE IN THE MORNING, GIVE THANKS
FOR THE FOOD AND FOR THE JOY OF LIVING."
— TECUMSEH

Date: _____

One moment that brought me peace today:
_____
_____
_____

One moment I am grateful for today:
_____
_____
_____

Date: _____

One moment that made me smile:
_____
_____
_____

One moment that I don't want to forget:
_____
_____
_____

"BETTER THAN A THOUSAND DAYS OF DILIGENT STUDY IS ONE DAY WITH A GREAT TEACHER."
— JAPANESE PROVERB

Date: _____

One moment that brought me joy today:
_____
_____
_____

One moment I am grateful for today:
_____
_____
_____

Date: _____

One moment that made me laugh:
_____
_____
_____

One moment that I don't want to forget:
_____
_____
_____

"LIVE A LIFE FULL OF HUMILITY, GRATITUDE, INTELLECTUAL CURIOSITY, AND NEVER STOP LEARNING." — GZA

Date: _____

One moment that brought me happiness today:
_____
_____
_____

One moment I am grateful for today:
_____
_____
_____

Date: _____

One moment that I am proud of:
_____
_____
_____

One moment that I don't want to forget:
_____
_____
_____

> "FOR ME, EVERY HOUR IS GRACE. AND I FEEL GRATITUDE IN MY HEART EACH TIME I CAN MEET SOMEONE AND LOOK AT HIS OR HER SMILE."
> — ELIE WIESEL

Date: _____

One moment that gave me hope today:
_____
_____
_____

One moment I am grateful for today:
_____
_____
_____

Date: _____

One moment that I treasured today:
_____
_____
_____

One moment that I don't want to forget:
_____
_____
_____

> "TEACHERS CAN CHANGE LIVES WITH JUST THE RIGHT MIX OF CHALK AND CHALLENGES."
> — JOYCE MEYER

Date: _____

One hope I have for my family is:
_____
_____
_____

One moment I am grateful for today:
_____
_____
_____

Date: _____

One dream I have for my family is:
_____
_____
_____

One moment that I don't want to forget:
_____
_____
_____

> "A TEACHER'S JOB IS TO TAKE A BUNCH OF LIVE WIRES AND SEE THAT THEY ARE WELL-GROUNDED."
> — DARWIN D. MARTIN

Date: _____

One moment that made me smile:
_____
_____
_____

One moment I am grateful for today:
_____
_____
_____

Date: _____

One moment that brought me joy today:
_____
_____
_____

One moment that I don't want to forget:
_____
_____
_____

> "STRIVE TO FIND THINGS TO BE THANKFUL FOR, AND JUST LOOK FOR THE GOOD IN WHO YOU ARE." — BETHANY HAMILTON

Date: _____

One moment that brought me comfort today
_____
_____
_____

One moment I am grateful for today:
_____
_____
_____

Date: _____

One moment that brought me happiness today:
_____
_____
_____

One moment that I don't want to forget:
_____
_____
_____

> "TEACHING IS A CALLING TOO. AND I'VE ALWAYS THOUGHT THAT TEACHERS IN THEIR WAY ARE HOLY—ANGELS LEADING THEIR FLOCKS OUT OF THE DARKNESS." — JEANNETTE WALLS

Date: _____

One moment that gave me confidence today:
_____
_____
_____

One moment I am grateful for today:
_____
_____
_____

Date: _____

One moment that brought me peace today:
_____
_____
_____

One moment that I don't want to forget:
_____
_____
_____

"THANKFULNESS IS THE QUICKEST PATH TO JOY."
— JEFFERSON BETHKE

Date: _____

One moment that made me laugh:
_____
_____
_____

One moment I am grateful for today:
_____
_____
_____

Date: _____

One moment that brought me comfort today:
_____
_____
_____

One moment that I don't want to forget:
_____
_____
_____

"REFLECT UPON YOUR PRESENT BLESSINGS, OF WHICH EVERY MAN HAS PLENTY; NOT ON YOUR PAST MISFORTUNES, OF WHICH ALL MEN HAVE SOME." — CHARLES DICKENS

Date: _____

One dream I have for my family is:
_____
_____
_____

One moment I am grateful for today:
_____
_____
_____

Date: _____

One moment that gave me hope today:
_____
_____
_____

One moment that I don't want to forget:
_____
_____
_____

> "YOUR HEART IS SLIGHTLY LARGER THAN THE AVERAGE HUMAN HEART, BUT THAT'S BECAUSE YOU'RE A TEACHER." — AARON BACALL

Date: _____

One moment that I am proud of:
_____
_____
_____

One moment I am grateful for today:
_____
_____
_____

Date: _____

One moment that gave me confidence today:
_____
_____
_____

One moment that I don't want to forget:
_____
_____
_____

> "WHEN I STARTED COUNTING MY BLESSINGS, MY WHOLE LIFE TURNED AROUND." — WILLIE NELSON

Date: _____

One dream I have for my family Is:
_____
_____
_____

One moment I am grateful for today:
_____
_____
_____

Date: _____

One moment that I am proud of:
_____
_____
_____

One moment that I don't want to forget:
_____
_____
_____

"TEACHING IS THE GREATEST ACT OF OPTIMISM."
— COLLEEN WILCOX

Date: _____

One moment that gave me hope today:
_____
_____
_____

One moment I am grateful for today:
_____
_____
_____

Date: _____

One moment that made me smile:
_____
_____
_____

One moment that I don't want to forget:
_____
_____
_____

> "STUDENTS DON'T CARE HOW MUCH YOU KNOW
> UNTIL THEY KNOW HOW MUCH YOU CARE."
> — JOHN C. MAXWELL

Date: _____

One moment that brought me joy today:
_____
_____
_____

One moment I am grateful for today:
_____
_____
_____

Date: _____

One moment that I am proud of:
_____
_____
_____

One moment that I don't want to forget:
_____
_____
_____

"IT IS NOT WHAT IS POURED INTO THE STUDENT,
BUT WHAT IS PLANTED, THAT COUNTS."
— E.P. BERTIN

Date: _____

One moment that gave me hope today:
_____
_____
_____

One moment I am grateful for today:
_____
_____
_____

Date: _____

One moment that made me laugh:
_____
_____
_____

One moment that I don't want to forget:
_____
_____
_____

> "THOSE WHO KNOW, DO. THOSE THAT UNDERSTAND, TEACH." — ARISTOTLE

Date: _____

One moment that brought me happiness today:
_____
_____
_____

One moment I am grateful for today:
_____
_____
_____

Date: _____

One moment that brought me joy today:
_____
_____
_____

One moment that I don't want to forget:
_____
_____
_____

> "I WOULD MAINTAIN THAT THANKS ARE THE HIGHEST FORM OF THOUGHT; AND THAT GRATITUDE IS HAPPINESS DOUBLED BY WONDER."
> — G.K. CHESTERTON

Date: _____

One moment that brought me comfort today:
_____
_____
_____

One moment I am grateful for today:
_____
_____
_____

Date: _____

One dream I have for my family is:
_____
_____
_____

One moment that I don't want to forget:
_____
_____
_____

> "PIGLET NOTICED THAT EVEN THOUGH HE HAD A VERY SMALL HEART, IT COULD HOLD A RATHER LARGE AMOUNT OF GRATITUDE." — A.A. MILNE

Date: _____

One moment that made me smile:
_____
_____
_____

One moment I am grateful for today:
_____
_____
_____

Date: _____

One moment that brought me peace today:
_____
_____
_____

One moment that I don't want to forget:
_____
_____
_____

> "THE FUNCTION OF EDUCATION IS TO TEACH ONE TO THINK INTENSIVELY AND TO THINK CRITICALLY. INTELLIGENCE PLUS CHARACTER—THAT IS THE GOAL OF TRUE EDUCATION." — MARTIN LUTHER KING, JR.

Date: _____

One moment that made me laugh:
_____
_____
_____

One moment I am grateful for today:
_____
_____
_____

Date: _____

One moment that brought me comfort today:
_____
_____
_____

One moment that I don't want to forget:
_____
_____
_____

> "THE BEST TEACHERS ARE THE ONES THAT CHANGE THEIR MINDS." — TERRY HEICK

Date: _____

One dream I have for my family is:
_____
_____
_____

One moment I am grateful for today:
_____
_____
_____

Date: _____

One moment that gave me hope today:
_____
_____
_____

One moment that I don't want to forget:
_____
_____
_____

"IT IS THE SUPREME ART OF THE TEACHER TO AWAKEN JOY IN CREATIVE EXPRESSION AND KNOWLEDGE." — ALBERT EINSTEIN

Date: _____

One moment that I am proud of:
_____
_____
_____

One moment I am grateful for today:
_____
_____
_____

Date: _____

One moment that gave me confidence today:
_____
_____
_____

One moment that I don't want to forget:
_____
_____
_____

"IN ORDINARY LIFE, WE HARDLY REALIZE THAT WE RECEIVE A GREAT DEAL MORE THAN WE GIVE, AND THAT IT IS ONLY WITH GRATITUDE THAT LIFE BECOMES RICH." — DIETRICH BONHOEFFER

Date: _____

One moment that brought me peace today:
_____
_____
_____

One moment I am grateful for today:
_____
_____
_____

Date: _____

One moment that made me smile:
_____
_____
_____

One moment that I don't want to forget:
_____
_____
_____

> "TRUE FORGIVENESS IS WHEN YOU CAN SAY, 'THANK YOU FOR THE EXPERIENCE.'"
> — OPRAH WINFREY

Date: _____

One moment that brought me joy today:
_____
_____
_____

One moment I am grateful for today:
_____
_____

Date: _____

One moment that made me laugh:
_____
_____
_____

One moment that I don't want to forget:
_____
_____
_____

> "GRATITUDE LOOKS TO THE PAST AND LOVE TO THE PRESENT; FEAR, AVARICE, LUST, AND AMBITION LOOK AHEAD." — C.S. LEWIS

Date: _____

One moment that brought me happiness today:
_____
_____
_____

One moment I am grateful for today:
_____
_____
_____

Date: _____

One moment that I am proud of:
_____
_____
_____

One moment that I don't want to forget:
_____
_____
_____

> "ONE CHILD, ONE TEACHER, ONE BOOK, AND ONE PEN CAN CHANGE THE WORLD."
> — MALALA YOUSAFZAI

Date: _____

One moment that gave me hope today:
_____
_____
_____

One moment I am grateful for today:
_____
_____
_____

Date: _____

One dream I have for my family is:
_____
_____
_____

One moment that I don't want to forget:
_____
_____
_____

> "I LIE IN BED AT NIGHT, AFTER ENDING MY PRAYERS WITH THE WORDS 'ICH DANKE DIR FÜR ALL DAS GUTE UND LIEBE UND SCHÖNE.' (THANK YOU, GOD, FOR ALL THAT IS GOOD AND DEAR AND BEAUTIFUL)" — ANNE FRANK

Date: _____

One moment that made me smile:
_____
_____
_____

One moment I am grateful for today:
_____
_____
_____

Date: _____

One moment that brought me joy today:
_____
_____
_____

One moment that I don't want to forget:
_____
_____
_____

"EDUCATION DOESN'T JUST MAKE US SMARTER
IT MAKES US WHOLE." — JILL BIDEN

Date: _____

One moment that brought me comfort today:
_____
_____
_____

One moment I am grateful for today:
_____
_____
_____

Date: _____

One moment that brought me happiness today:
_____
_____
_____

One moment that I don't want to forget:
_____
_____
_____

"GRATITUDE BESTOWS REVERENCE...CHANGING FOREVER HOW WE EXPERIENCE LIFE AND THE WORLD." — JOHN MILTON

Date: _____

One moment that gave me confidence today:
_____
_____
_____

One moment I am grateful for today:
_____
_____
_____

Date: _____

One moment that brought me peace today:
_____
_____
_____

One moment that I don't want to forget:
_____
_____
_____

> "APPRECIATION CAN MAKE A DAY, EVEN CHANGE A LIFE. YOUR WILLINGNESS TO PUT IT INTO WORDS IS ALL THAT IS NECESSARY."
> — MARGARET COUSINS

Date: _____

One moment that made me laugh:
_____
_____
_____

One moment I am grateful for today:
_____
_____
_____

Date: _____

One moment that brought me comfort today:
_____
_____
_____

One moment that I don't want to forget:
_____
_____
_____

"THE FACT THAT YOU WORRY ABOUT BEING A GOOD TEACHER, MEANS THAT YOU ALREADY ARE ONE." — JODI PICOULT

Date: _____

One dream I have for my family is:
_____
_____
_____

One moment I am grateful for today:
_____
_____
_____

Date: _____

One moment that gave me hope today:
_____
_____
_____

One moment that I don't want to forget:
_____
_____
_____

> "A WELL EDUCATED MIND WILL ALWAYS HAVE MORE QUESTIONS THAN ANSWERS."
> — HELEN KELLER

Date: _____

One moment that I am proud of:
_____
_____
_____

One moment I am grateful for today:
_____
_____
_____

Date: _____

One moment that gave me confidence today:
_____
_____
_____

One moment that I don't want to forget:
_____
_____
_____

> "FOR MY PART, I AM ALMOST CONTENTED JUST NOW, AND VERY THANKFUL. GRATITUDE IS A DIVINE EMOTION: IT FILLS THE HEART, BUT NOT TO BURSTING; IT WARMS IT, BUT NOT TO FEVER."
> — CHARLOTTE BRONTË

Date: _____

One moment that brought me peace today:
_____
_____
_____

One moment I am grateful for today:
_____
_____
_____

Date: _____

One moment that made me smile:
_____
_____
_____

One moment that I don't want to forget:
_____
_____
_____

"HE IS A WISE MAN WHO DOES NOT GRIEVE FOR THE THINGS WHICH HE HAS NOT, BUT REJOICES FOR THOSE WHICH HE HAS." — EPICTETUS

Date: _____

One moment that brought me joy today:
_____
_____
_____

One moment I am grateful for today:
_____
_____
_____

Date: _____

One moment that made me laugh:
_____
_____
_____

One moment that I don't want to forget:
_____
_____
_____

"OUR FINGERPRINTS DON'T FADE FROM THE LIVES WE TOUCH." — JUDY BLUME

Date: _____

One moment that brought me happiness today:
_____
_____
_____

One moment I am grateful for today:
_____
_____
_____

Date: _____

One moment that I am proud of:
_____
_____
_____

One moment that I don't want to forget:
_____
_____
_____

"THE MEANING OF LIFE IS TO FIND YOUR GIFT. THE
PURPOSE OF LIFE IS TO GIVE IT AWAY."
— PABLO PICASSO

Date: _____

One moment that gave me hope today:
_____
_____
_____

One moment I am grateful for today:
_____
_____
_____

Date: _____

One dream I have for my family is:
_____
_____
_____

One moment that I don't want to forget:
_____
_____
_____

> "DO NOT SPOIL WHAT YOU HAVE BY DESIRING WHAT YOU HAVE NOT; REMEMBER THAT WHAT YOU NOW HAVE WAS ONCE AMONG THE THINGS YOU ONLY HOPED FOR" — EPICURUS

Date: _____

One moment that made me smile:
_____
_____
_____

One moment I am grateful for today:
_____
_____
_____

Date: _____

One moment that brought me joy today:
_____
_____
_____

One moment that I don't want to forget:
_____
_____
_____

> "WHEN ONE TEACHES, TWO LEARN."
> — ROBERT HEINLEIN

Date: _____

One moment that brought me comfort today:
_____
_____
_____

One moment I am grateful for today:
_____
_____
_____

Date: _____

One moment that brought me happiness today:
_____
_____
_____

One moment that I don't want to forget:
_____
_____
_____

"I CANNOT TEACH ANYBODY ANYTHING, I CAN ONLY MAKE THEM THINK." — SOCRATES

Date: _____

One moment that gave me confidence today:
_____
_____
_____

One moment I am grateful for today:
_____
_____
_____

Date: _____

One moment that brought me peace today:
_____
_____
_____

One moment that I don't want to forget:
_____
_____
_____

"TEACHERS TEACH SOMEONE SOMETHING, IN THAT ORDER" — SAMUEL NATALE

Date: _____

One moment that made me laugh:
_____
_____
_____

One moment I am grateful for today:
_____
_____
_____

Date: _____

One moment that brought me comfort today:
_____
_____
_____

One moment that I don't want to forget:
_____
_____
_____

"IF THE ONLY PRAYER YOU SAID WAS THANK YOU, THAT WOULD BE ENOUGH." — MEISTER ECKHART

Date: _____

One dream I have for my family is:
_____
_____
_____

One moment I am grateful for today:
_____
_____
_____

Date: _____

One moment that gave me hope today:
_____
_____
_____

One moment that I don't want to forget:
_____
_____
_____

"I CANNOT BE A TEACHER WITHOUT EXPOSING WHO I AM." — PAULO FREIRE

Date: _____

One moment that I am proud of:
_____
_____
_____

One moment I am grateful for today:
_____
_____
_____

Date: _____

One moment that gave me confidence today:
_____
_____
_____

One moment that I don't want to forget:
_____
_____
_____

> "IN A COMPLETELY RATIONAL SOCIETY, THE BEST OF US WOULD BE TEACHERS AND THE REST OF US WOULD HAVE TO SETTLE FOR SOMETHING ELSE."
> — LEE IACOCCA

Date: _____

One moment that brought me peace today:
_____
_____
_____

One moment I am grateful for today:
_____
_____
_____

Date: _____

One moment that made me smile:
_____
_____
_____

One moment that I don't want to forget:
_____
_____
_____

"WHEN I PRAY, I ALWAYS THANK MOTHER NATURE FOR ALL THE BEAUTY IN THE WORLD. IT'S ABOUT HAVING AN ATTITUDE OF GRATITUDE."
— MIRANDA KERR

Date: _____

One moment that brought me joy today:
_____
_____
_____

One moment I am grateful for today:
_____
_____
_____

Date: _____

One moment that made me laugh:
_____
_____
_____

One moment that I don't want to forget:
_____
_____
_____

"GRATITUDE IS RICHES. COMPLAIN IS POVERTY."
— DORIS DAY

Date: _____

One moment that brought me happiness today:
_____
_____
_____

One moment I am grateful for today:
_____
_____

Date: _____

One moment that I am proud of:
_____
_____
_____

One moment that I don't want to forget:
_____
_____
_____

> "THE MEDIOCRE TEACHER TELLS. THE GOOD TEACHER EXPLAINS. THE SUPERIOR TEACHER DEMONSTRATES. THE GREAT TEACHER INSPIRES."
> — WILLIAM ARTHUR WARD

Date: _____

One moment that gave me hope today:
_____
_____
_____

One moment I am grateful for today:
_____
_____
_____

Date: _____

One dream I have for my family is:
_____
_____
_____

One moment that I don't want to forget:
_____
_____
_____

"THIS IS A WONDERFUL DAY I HAVE NEVER SEEN THIS ONE BEFORE." — MAYA ANGELOU

Date: _____

One moment that made me smile:
_____
_____
_____

One moment I am grateful for today:
_____
_____
_____

Date: _____

One moment that brought me joy today:
_____
_____
_____

One moment that I don't want to forget:
_____
_____
_____

> "A GOOD TEACHER IS LIKE A CANDLE – IT CONSUMES ITSELF TO LIGHT THE WAY FOR OTHERS." — MUSTAFA KEMAL ATATÜRK

Date: _____

One moment that brought me comfort today:
_____
_____
_____

One moment I am grateful for today:
_____
_____
_____

Date: _____

One moment that brought me happiness today:
_____
_____
_____

One moment that I don't want to forget:
_____
_____
_____

> "WE LEARNED ABOUT GRATITUDE AND HUMILITY – THAT SO MANY PEOPLE HAD A HAND IN OUR SUCCESS." — MICHELLE OBAMA

Date: _____

One moment that gave me confidence today:
_____
_____
_____

One moment I am grateful for today:
_____
_____
_____

Date: _____

One moment that brought me peace today:
_____
_____
_____

One moment that I don't want to forget:
_____
_____
_____

"TEACHING IS THE ONE PROFESSION THAT CREATES ALL OTHER PROFESSIONS." — UNKNOWN

Date: _____

One moment that made me laugh:
_____
_____
_____

One moment I am grateful for today:
_____
_____
_____

Date: _____

One moment that brought me comfort today:
_____
_____
_____

One moment that I don't want to forget:
_____
_____
_____

> "LET GRATITUDE BE THE PILLOW UPON WHICH YOU KNEEL TO SAY YOUR NIGHTLY PRAYER. AND LET FAITH BE THE BRIDGE YOU BUILD TO OVERCOME EVIL AND WELCOME GOOD." — MAYA ANGELOU

Date: _____

One dream I have for my family is:
_____
_____
_____

One moment I am grateful for today:
_____
_____
_____

Date: _____

One moment that gave me hope today:
_____
_____
_____

One moment that I don't want to forget:
_____
_____
_____

"THE SOUL THAT GIVES THANKS CAN FIND COMFORT IN EVERYTHING; THE SOUL THAT COMPLAINS CAN FIND COMFORT IN NOTHING."
— HANNAH WHITALL SMITH

Date: _____

One moment that I am proud of:
_____
_____
_____

One moment I am grateful for today:
_____
_____
_____

Date: _____

One moment that gave me confidence today:
_____
_____
_____

One moment that I don't want to forget:
_____
_____
_____

> "THE JOB OF AN EDUCATOR IS TO TEACH STUDENTS TO SEE VITALITY IN THEMSELVES."
> — JOSEPH CAMPBELL

Date: _____

One moment that brought me peace today:
_____
_____
_____

One moment I am grateful for today:
_____
_____
_____

Date: _____

One moment that made me smile:
_____
_____
_____

One moment that I don't want to forget:
_____
_____
_____

"TO KNOW HOW TO SUGGEST IS THE ART OF TEACHING." — HENRI-FRÉDÉRIC AMIEL

Date: _____

One moment that brought me joy today:
_____
_____
_____

One moment I am grateful for today:
_____
_____
_____

Date: _____

One moment that made me laugh:
_____
_____
_____

One moment that I don't want to forget:
_____
_____
_____

"REST AND BE THANKFUL."
— WILLIAM WORDSWORTH

Date: _____

One moment that brought me happiness today:
_____
_____
_____

One moment I am grateful for today:
_____
_____
_____

Date: _____

One moment that I am proud of:
_____
_____
_____

One moment that I don't want to forget:
_____
_____
_____

"GRATITUDE IS THE SIGN OF NOBLE SOULS."
— AESOP

Date: _____

One moment that gave me hope today:
_____
_____
_____

One moment I am grateful for today:
_____
_____
_____

Date: _____

One dream I have for my family is:
_____
_____
_____

One moment that I don't want to forget:
_____
_____
_____

> "THE GREATEST SIGN OF SUCCESS FOR A TEACHER IS TO BE ABLE TO SAY, 'THE CHILDREN ARE NOW WORKING AS IF I DID NOT EXIST.'"
> — MARIA MONTESSORI

Date: _____

One moment that made me smile:
_____
_____
_____

One moment I am grateful for today:
_____
_____
_____

Date: _____

One moment that brought me joy today:
_____
_____
_____

One moment that I don't want to forget:
_____
_____
_____

"ASK 'HOW WILL THEY LEARN BEST?' NOT 'CAN THEY LEARN?'" — JAMIE ESCALANTE

Date: _____

One moment that brought me comfort today:
_____
_____
_____

One moment I am grateful for today:
_____
_____
_____

Date: _____

One moment that brought me happiness today:
_____
_____
_____

One moment that I don't want to forget:
_____
_____
_____

> "FAR AND AWAY THE BEST PRIZE THAT LIFE OFFERS IS THE CHANCE TO WORK HARD AT WORK WORTH DOING." — THEODORE ROOSEVELT

Date: _____

One moment that gave me confidence today:
_____
_____
_____

One moment I am grateful for today:
_____
_____
_____

Date: _____

One moment that brought me peace today:
_____
_____
_____

One moment that I don't want to forget:
_____
_____
_____

"I AWOKE THIS MORNING WITH DEVOUT THANKSGIVING FOR MY FRIENDS, THE OLD AND THE NEW." — RALPH WALDO EMERSON

Date: _____

One moment that made me laugh:
_____
_____
_____

One moment I am grateful for today:
_____
_____
_____

Date: _____

One moment that brought me comfort today:
_____
_____
_____

One moment that I don't want to forget:
_____
_____
_____

> "I'M STILL THANKING ALL THE STARS, ONE BY ONE." — MARISSA MEYER

Date: _____

One dream I have for my family is:
_____
_____
_____

One moment I am grateful for today:
_____
_____
_____

Date: _____

One moment that gave me hope today:
_____
_____
_____

One moment that I don't want to forget:
_____
_____
_____

"TEACHING MIGHT EVEN BE THE GREATEST OF THE ARTS SINCE THE MEDIUM IS THE HUMAN MIND AND SPIRIT." — JOHN STEINBECK

Date: _____

One moment that I am proud of:
_____
_____
_____

One moment I am grateful for today:
_____
_____
_____

Date: _____

One moment that gave me confidence today:
_____
_____
_____

One moment that I don't want to forget:
_____
_____
_____

"WHEN EATING FRUIT, REMEMBER THE
ONE WHO PLANTED THE TREE."
— VIETNAMESE PROVERB

Date: _____

One moment that brought me peace today:
_____
_____
_____

One moment I am grateful for today:
_____
_____
_____

Date: _____

One moment that made me smile:
_____
_____
_____

One moment that I don't want to forget:
_____
_____
_____

> "LISTENING IS THE MOST DIFFICULT SKILL TO LEARN AND THE MOST IMPORTANT TO HAVE."
> — AFRICAN PROVERB

Date: _____

One moment that brought me joy today:
_____
_____
_____

One moment I am grateful for today:
_____
_____
_____

Date: _____

One moment that made me laugh:
_____
_____
_____

One moment that I don't want to forget:
_____
_____
_____

> "GRATITUDE IS A QUALITY SIMILAR TO ELECTRICITY:
> IT MUST BE PRODUCED AND DISCHARGED
> AND USED UP IN ORDER TO EXIST AT ALL."
> — WILLIAM FAULKNER

Date: _____

One dream I have for my family is:
_____
_____
_____

One moment I am grateful for today:
_____
_____
_____

Date: _____

One moment that I am proud of:
_____
_____
_____

One moment that I don't want to forget:
_____
_____
_____

> "EDUCATION IS NOT PREPARATION FOR LIFE;
> EDUCATION IS LIFE ITSELF." — JOHN DEWEY

Date: _____

One moment that gave me hope today:
_____
_____
_____

One moment I am grateful for today:
_____
_____
_____

Date: _____

One dream I have for my family is:
_____
_____
_____

One moment that I don't want to forget:
_____
_____
_____

> "WHEN YOU ARE GRATEFUL, FEAR DISAPPEARS AND ABUNDANCE APPEARS." — ANTHONY ROBBINS

Date: _____

One moment that made me smile:
_____
_____
_____

One moment I am grateful for today:
_____
_____
_____

GIVE THANKS WITH A GRATEFUL HEART,
ON THESE DAYS AND ALWAYS.

Made in the USA
Monee, IL
11 February 2022